REUDOR's THE DOODLE FAMILY™

the Hebrew Letters tell their Story

Verse: Reudor   Art: Jack Knight, Reudor, Burt Griswold

PITSPOPANY
NEW YORK♦JERUSALEM

Published by Pitspopany Press

PITSPOPANY PRESS books may be purchased for educational or special sales by contacting:
Marketing Director, Pitspopany Press, 40 East 78th Street, New York, New York 10021.
Tel: (800) 232-2931 Fax: (212) 472-6253

Hardcover ISBN: 0-943706-24-6
Softcover ISBN: 0-943706-23-8

Printed in Hong Kong

Where to Find What

Alef

Look down in the ocean,
Do you see it? What is it?
It's the Island of Alef,
Let's go for a visit!
You can come here by ship
Or on board a red plane,
But you can't ride a bike
Or a train - that's insane!

You can eat nuts and peaches
And big purple pears,
Play ball with a lion
And race with wild hares.
You can juggle pink grapefruits
Way up in the air,
On the Island of Alef
You can do what you dare!

Bet

How can this be?
How can this be?
A dog builds a house
Way up in a tree?
"I think it's preposterous!"
Huffed the baboon
"It could be disastrous!"
Warned the loon.

The panther just frowned
The duck he just quacked
The thrush nearly cried,
"This dog must be cracked!"
The beaver looked up, asking
"What's wrong with you?"
But Poodly just smiled,
And said, "I love the view!"

He's playing guitar
While eating ice cream,
This camel's a star,
And I think he's a scream!
There's a roof on his head
In case it should rain,
If he falls overboard
He'll just climb up again!

He's surfing the wave,
while smelling a daisy,
Do you think he's brave?
Do you think he's crazy?
With a goat and a seal,
He is riding the surf,
Now he's doing a cartwheel -
This camel's got nerve!

Dalet

What's on the other
Side of the door?
There may be a movie,
Or a candy store,
A bear eating honey
Inside a beehive,
Or a squirrel and a bunny
Clapping high-five?

Now just close your eyes
And go ring the bell,
Here's a surprise -
A real magic spell!
From ceiling to floor
It is swimming with fish!
Behind this door
Is anything you wish.

Hey

"Hey, hey, hey!
Could you please stop?
Do you know the way
To the mountain top?"
"It's way up there
Just past that cloud
I hope there's room there
For all of your crowd.

Hey, hey, hey!
When you get to the top
Are you going to play?
Will you drink soda pop?"
"We did not come to stay,
We are just passing by,
We just can't find the way
Down this mountain high..."

Vav

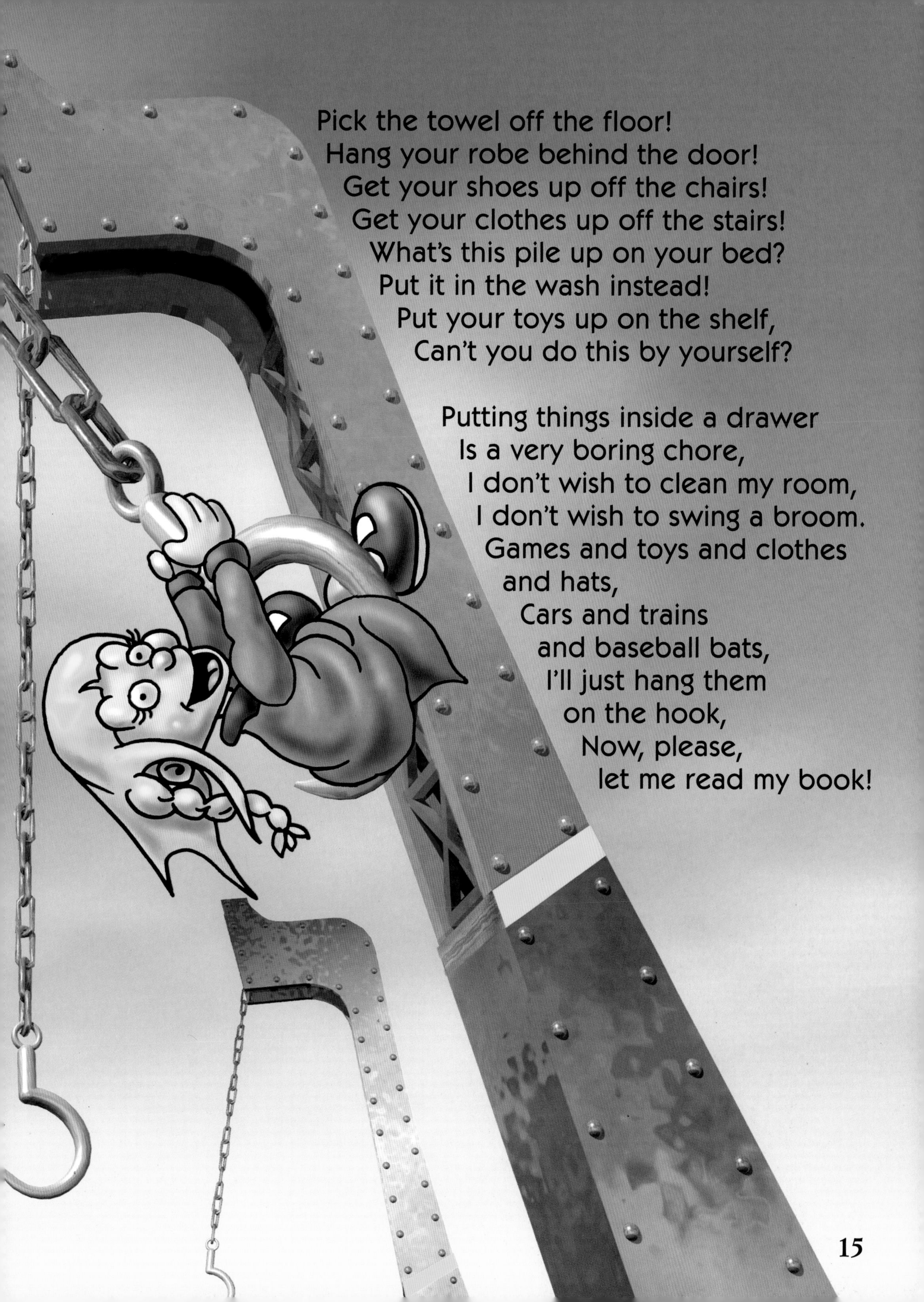

Pick the towel off the floor!
Hang your robe behind the door!
Get your shoes up off the chairs!
Get your clothes up off the stairs!
What's this pile up on your bed?
Put it in the wash instead!
Put your toys up on the shelf,
Can't you do this by yourself?

Putting things inside a drawer
Is a very boring chore,
I don't wish to clean my room,
I don't wish to swing a broom.
Games and toys and clothes
and hats,
Cars and trains
and baseball bats,
I'll just hang them
on the hook,
Now, please,
let me read my book!

Zayin

In the middle of the night,
In the darkest of the dark,
Suddenly there was a light,
Suddenly there was a spark.
It was glowing like a flame,
It was shining, burning bright,
Nothing seemed to be the same
As the darkness turned to light.

"It looks so strange, it feels so weird,
Zady, can you tell us why?"
Smiling, Grandpa stroked his beard,
The flame was sparkling in his eye,
"If you get lost it finds your place,
It warms you up when you are cold,
It gives your smile a happy face,
And all you touch it turns to gold."

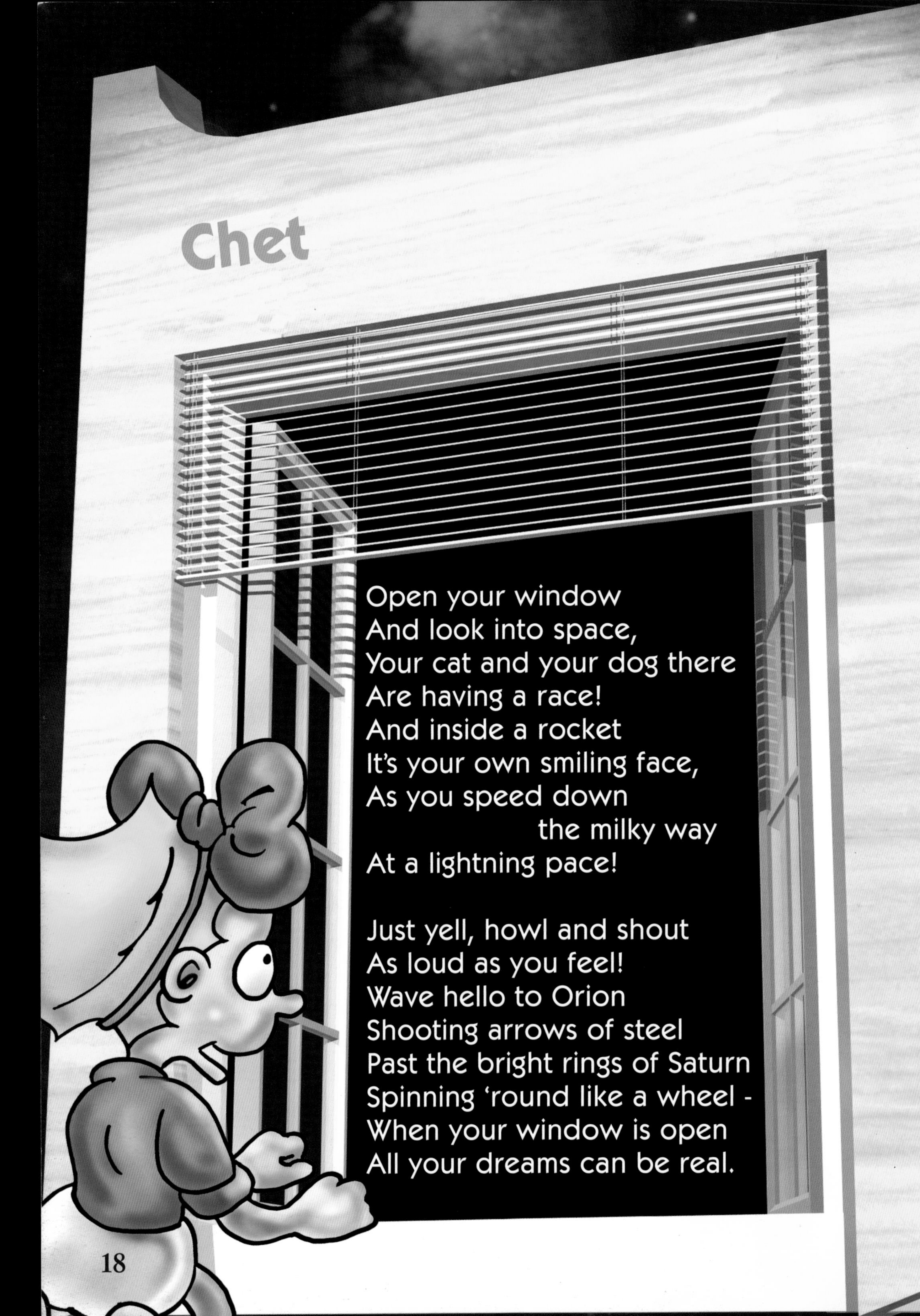

Chet

Open your window
And look into space,
Your cat and your dog there
Are having a race!
And inside a rocket
It's your own smiling face,
As you speed down
the milky way
At a lightning pace!

Just yell, howl and shout
As loud as you feel!
Wave hello to Orion
Shooting arrows of steel
Past the bright rings of Saturn
Spinning 'round like a wheel -
When your window is open
All your dreams can be real.

Tet

My little lamb
Has run away,
She simply ran
And wouldn't stay.
She raced down the valley,
I chased her up hill,
I chased her all day
But she wouldn't stay still.

I asked a pilot
Flying by,
"Can you see her
From the sky?"
"She ate the baker's
Yummy cake,
And now she has
A tummy ache!"

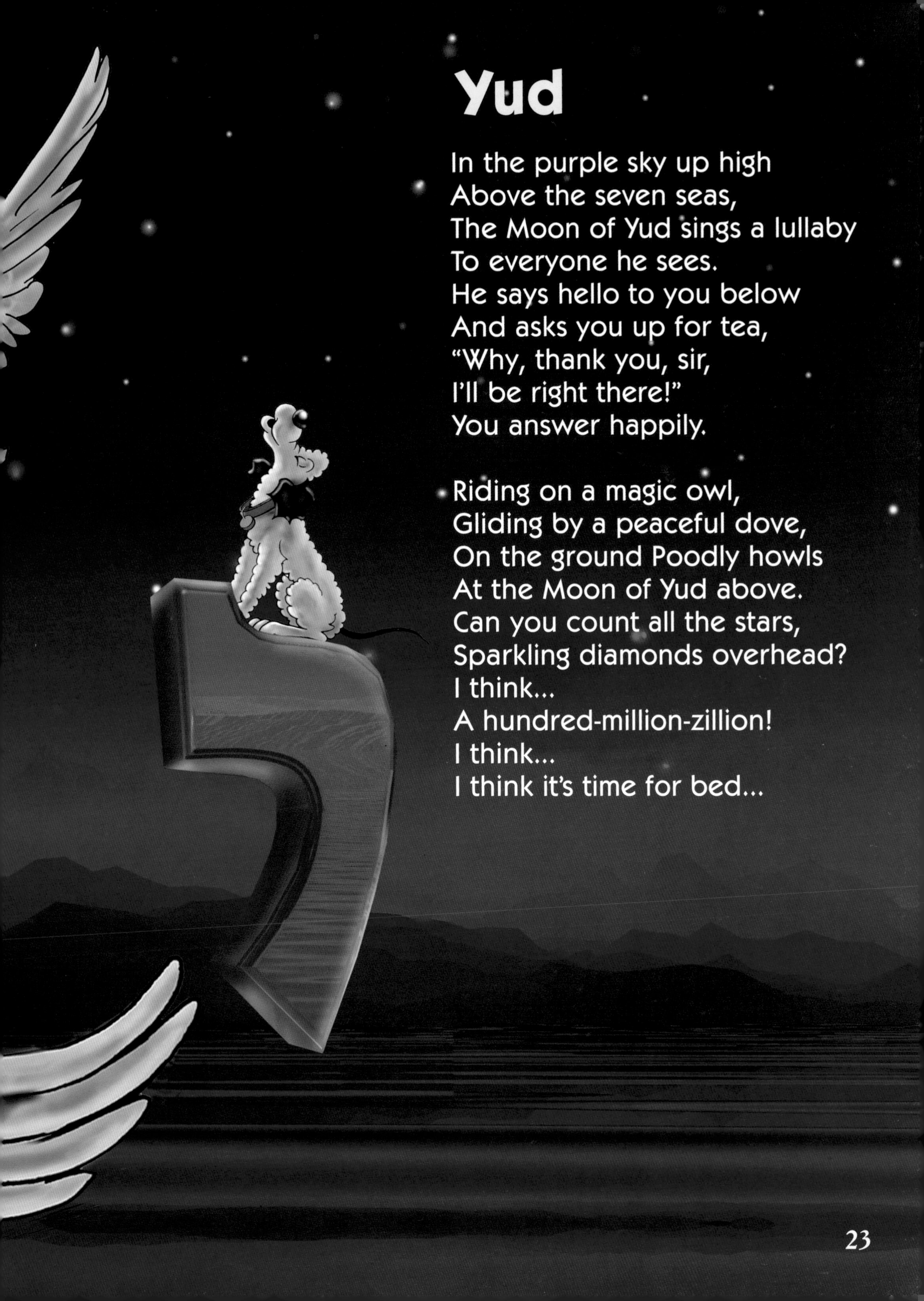

Yud

In the purple sky up high
Above the seven seas,
The Moon of Yud sings a lullaby
To everyone he sees.
He says hello to you below
And asks you up for tea,
"Why, thank you, sir,
I'll be right there!"
You answer happily.

Riding on a magic owl,
Gliding by a peaceful dove,
On the ground Poodly howls
At the Moon of Yud above.
Can you count all the stars,
Sparkling diamonds overhead?
I think...
A hundred-million-zillion!
I think...
I think it's time for bed...

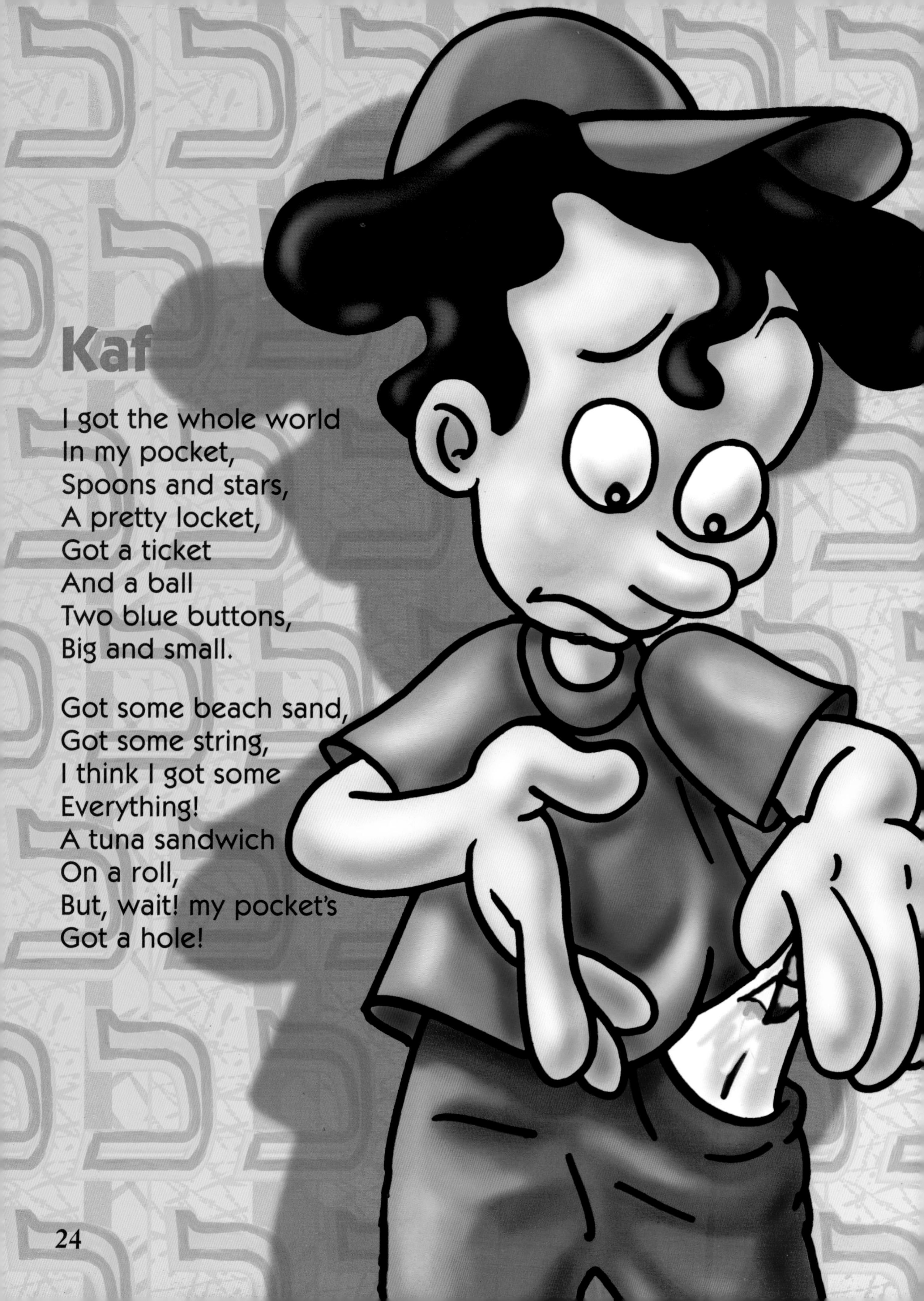

Kaf

I got the whole world
In my pocket,
Spoons and stars,
A pretty locket,
Got a ticket
And a ball
Two blue buttons,
Big and small.

Got some beach sand,
Got some string,
I think I got some
Everything!
A tuna sandwich
On a roll,
But, wait! my pocket's
Got a hole!

Lamed
ל

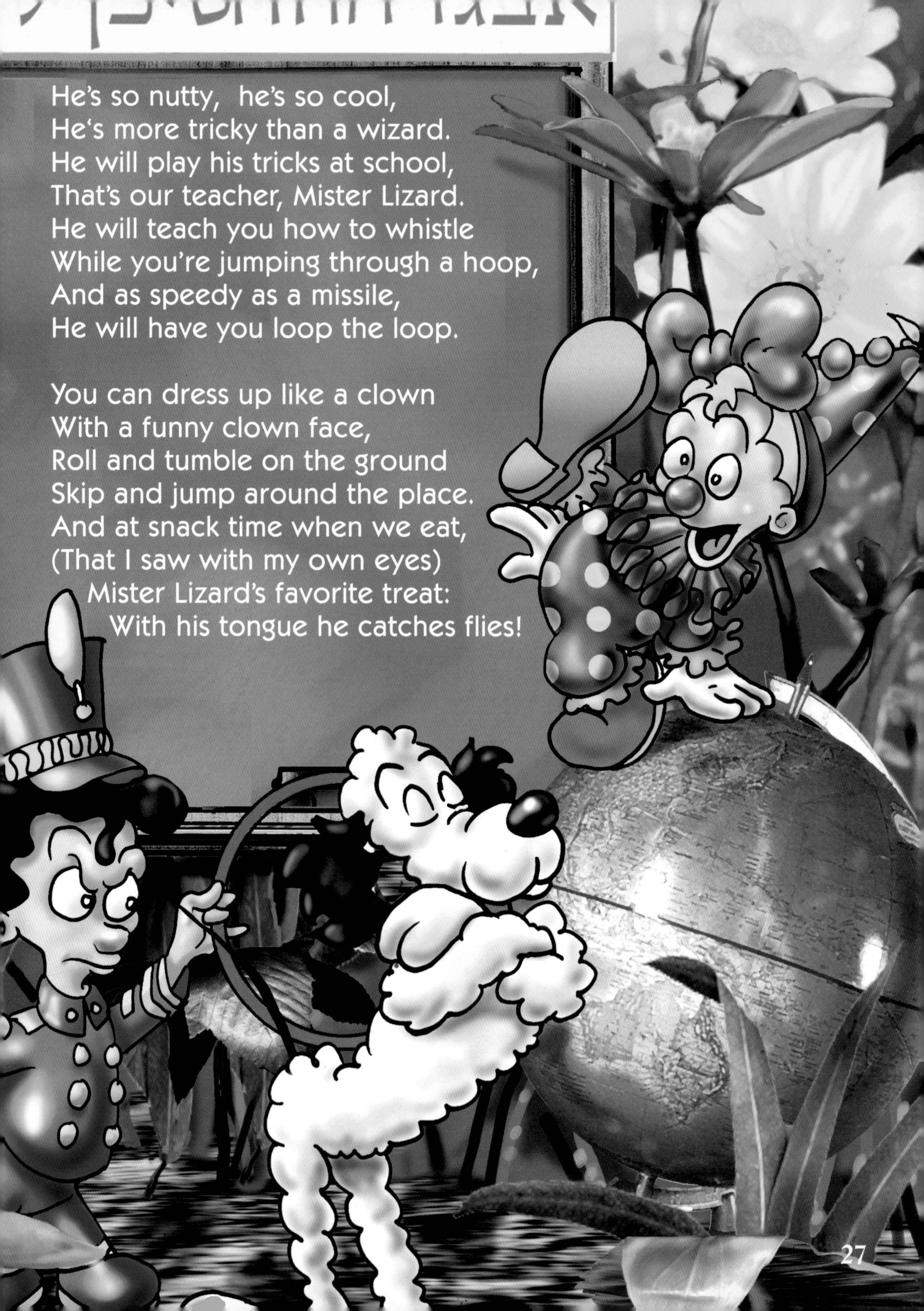

He's so nutty, he's so cool,
He's more tricky than a wizard.
He will play his tricks at school,
That's our teacher, Mister Lizard.
He will teach you how to whistle
While you're jumping through a hoop,
And as speedy as a missile,
He will have you loop the loop.

You can dress up like a clown
With a funny clown face,
Roll and tumble on the ground
Skip and jump around the place.
And at snack time when we eat,
(That I saw with my own eyes)
Mister Lizard's favorite treat:
With his tongue he catches flies!

Mem

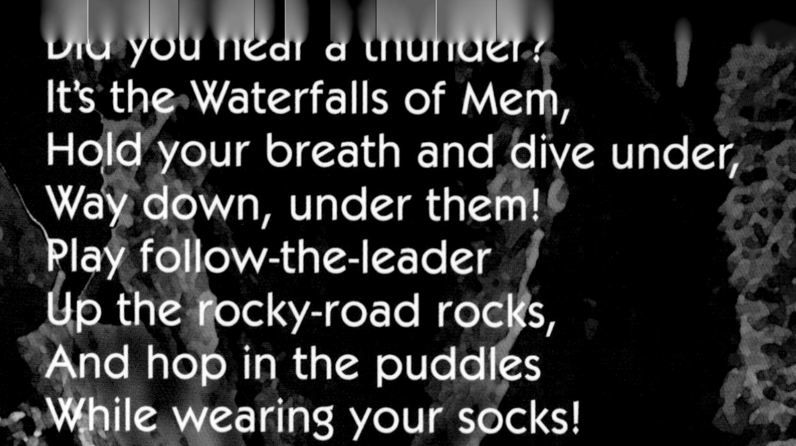

Did you hear a thunder?
It's the Waterfalls of Mem,
Hold your breath and dive under,
Way down, under them!
Play follow-the-leader
Up the rocky-road rocks,
And hop in the puddles
While wearing your socks!

You can hide-and-go-seek
Inside of a cave,
Ride the wild water slide
If you really feel brave.
Do three summersaults
While kicking and splashing,
You can stay wet all day
This place is just smashing!

a tempo
p

Nun

The Harp of Nun
Just loves to play
A happy tune
All night and day.
And you can help
And add a spark,
So howl and yelp
And even bark!

Don't have to sing
Just make some noise
Just twist and swing
And clank your toys.
Roar with the tiger,
Screech with the hawk,
Dance with the spider
Doing the
daddy-long-legs
walk!

Puffy, fluffy, floating free,
Cotton candy overhead,
Climb the ladder up and see
It's even softer than your bed.
Rocks as light as cotton balls,
Footsteps on a velvet rug,
Walk through clouds as thick as walls
Soft and safe as Grandma's hug.

Ride a horse across the plain,
Play with plushy purple squirrels,
Story books, a passing plane,
Sugar cubes as white as pearls.
Spinning dizzy on a draydel,
Bouncing gently on your head
Like a baby in a cradle,
It's even softer
than your bed.

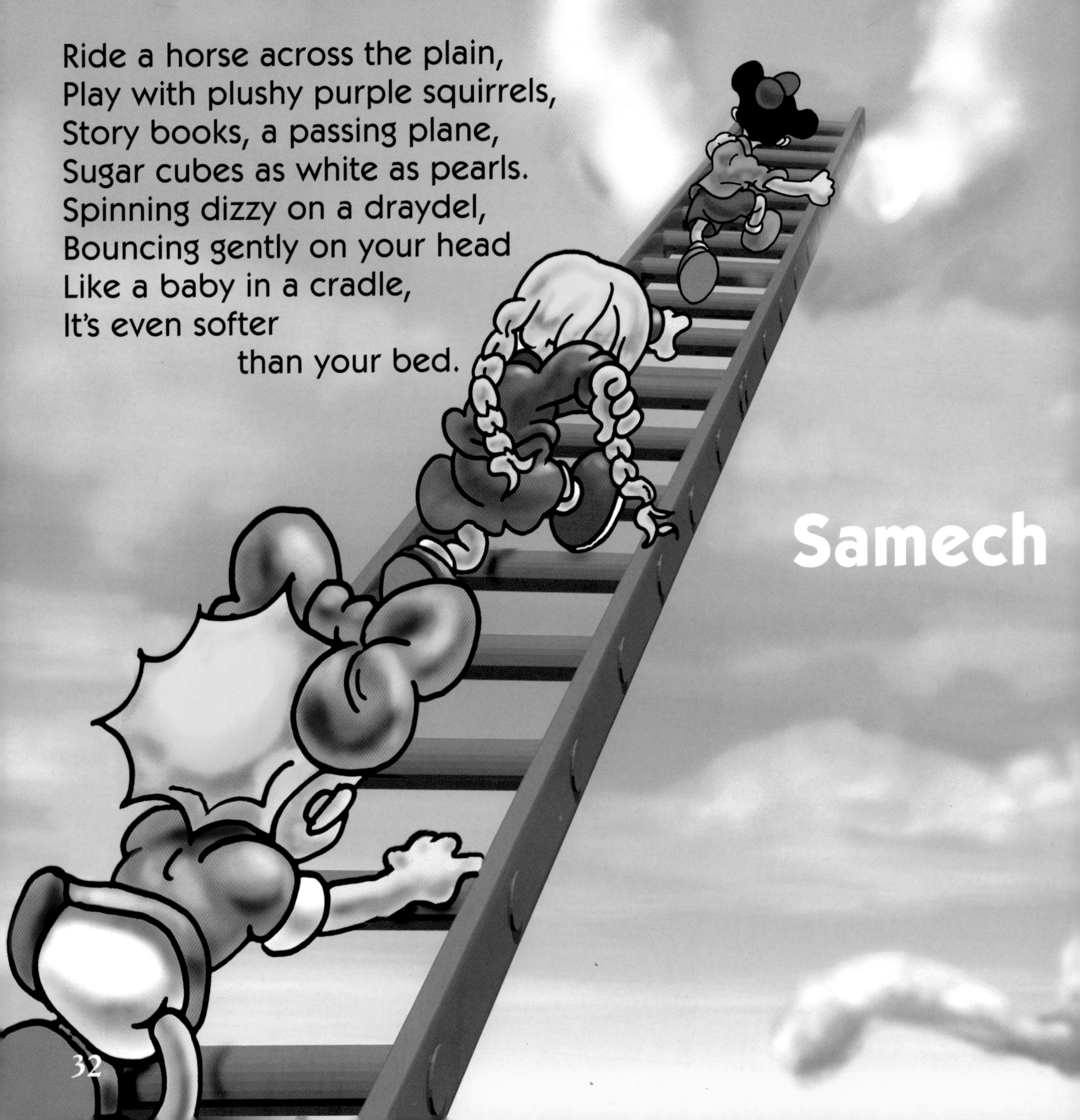

Samech

Ayin

The Eye can see
The clouds up high,
Across the sea
Can see the eye.
It sees the web
The spider weaves,
It sees the leaves
Upon the trees.

The eye can spy
Mice eating grapes,
And cakes, and pies
In funny shapes.
The eye sees bats
And flying crows,
Does it ever get tired?
Does it ever close?

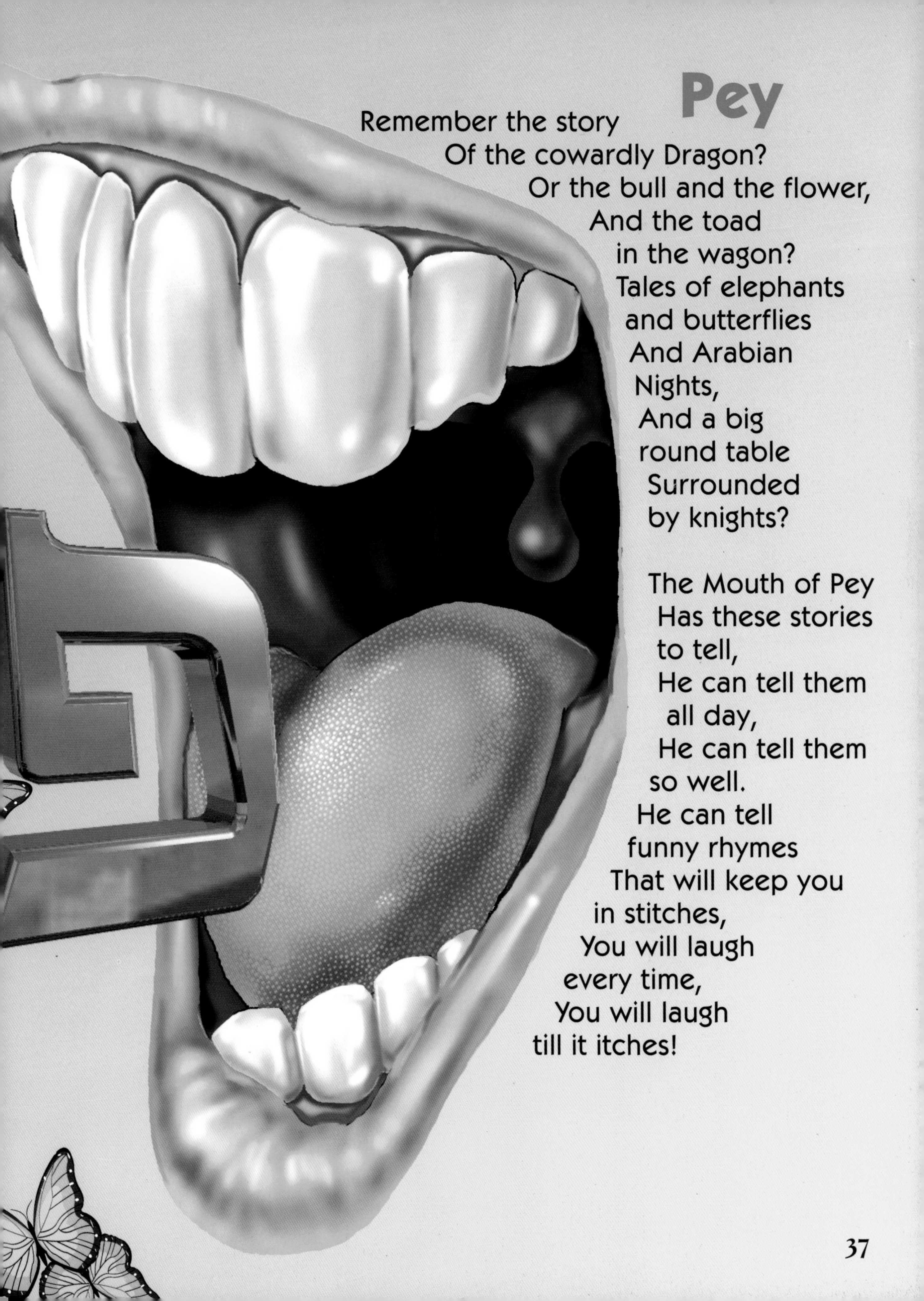

Pey

Remember the story
Of the cowardly Dragon?
Or the bull and the flower,
And the toad
in the wagon?
Tales of elephants
and butterflies
And Arabian
Nights,
And a big
round table
Surrounded
by knights?

The Mouth of Pey
Has these stories
to tell,
He can tell them
all day,
He can tell them
so well.
He can tell
funny rhymes
That will keep you
in stitches,
You will laugh
every time,
You will laugh
till it itches!

Tzadik

Come by ship,
Come by boat,
You can skydive,
You can float,
Ride a turtle
Or a frog,
Swim together
With your dog!

Take a breath
And come on under,
You will have
A lot of fun there!
From inside
The submarine
You'll see a world
All blue and green!

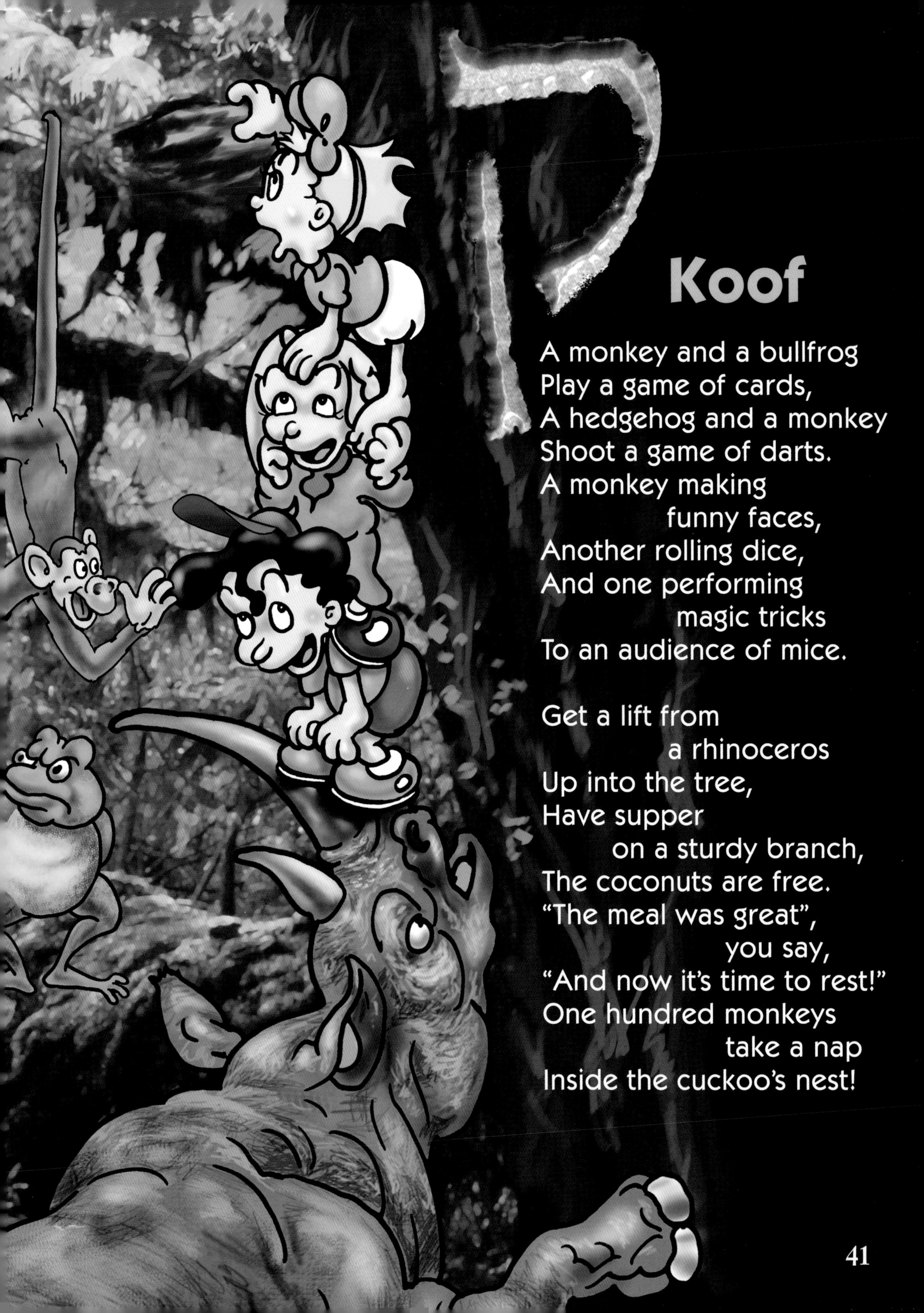

Koof

A monkey and a bullfrog
Play a game of cards,
A hedgehog and a monkey
Shoot a game of darts.
A monkey making
funny faces,
Another rolling dice,
And one performing
magic tricks
To an audience of mice.

Get a lift from
a rhinoceros
Up into the tree,
Have supper
on a sturdy branch,
The coconuts are free.
"The meal was great",
you say,
"And now it's time to rest!"
One hundred monkeys
take a nap
Inside the cuckoo's nest!

Raish

Listen to the wind blow,
People waiting for the rain,
Clouds line up in a row
Like a long and winding train.
Yes, our house is nice and warm,
But inside we will not stay,
We won't let a little storm
Keep us in the house all day!

We refuse to run and hide
On this stormy, windy day.
On the wind we'll take a ride,
Ride the wind up and away.
We don't mind if we get wet,
Buttoned up from head to toe,
We're all ready, we're all set,
On the wind we'll go, go, GO!

Silence is golden when I sleep
I don't want to hear a peep!
I don't want to hear you sing!
I don't want a bell to ring!
I don't wish to race a fox,
I don't wish to chase an ox.
Let me lie here in my bed,
With my blanket over head.

Shin

Don't smash hammer on a nail,
Keep as quiet as a snail,
Keep the sun behind my drapes,
Keep away those noisy apes.
HELP! This noise! This loud racket!
Someone's banging on a bucket?!
Don't alarm-clocks know the rule?
Today's Shabbat, we have no school!

Taf

I like it here
Under the palm,
It's shady and clear
And the air is calm.
But, look, a procession
Is heading this way!
I have the impression
They're coming to play!

A talking parrot
Saying hello,
A goat, a ferret,
A fat buffalo,
A marching band
Drumming Bim! Bam! Boom!
Could you give me a hand?
I'll need to make room!

the Hebrew Letters Spell Words

The Hebrew Letters		Magic numbers	Words, words, and more words!
א	Alef	1	Island (ee) אִי, Red (ah-dome) אָדֹם, Lion (ar-yeh) אַרְיֵה Airplane (avee-rone) אֲוִירוֹן, Ship (oh-nee-yah) אֳנִיָּה
ב	Bet	2	House (ba-yit) בַּיִת, Panther (bahr-de-lahs) בַּרְדְּלָס Duck (bahr-vahz) בַּרְוָז, Beaver (boh-neh) בּוֹנֶה
ג	Gimmel	3	Camel (gah-mal) גָּמָל, Ice cream (glee-dah) גְּלִידָה Surfboard (gahl-shahn) גַּלְשָׁן, Rain (geh-shem) גֶּשֶׁם
ד	Dalet	4	Door (deh-let) דֶּלֶת, Honey (dvahsh) דְּבַשׁ Bear (dohv) דֹּב, Fish (dahg) דָּג, Mail (doh-ahr) דֹּאַר
ה	Hey	5	Mountain (hahr) הַר, Crowd (hah-mone) הָמוֹן Parents (ho-reem) הוֹרִים, Show (hah-tzah-gah) הַצָּגָה
ו	Vav	6	Hook (vahv) וָו, Pink (vah-rode) וָרֹד Certainly (vah-die) וַדַּאי, Rose (veh-red) וֶרֶד
ז	Zayin	7	Gold (zah-hahv) זָהָב, Beard (zah-kahn) זָקָן Old (zah-ken) זָקֵן, Fly (zvoov) זְבוּב
ח	Chet	8	Space (chah-lahl) חָלָל, Window (chah-lone) חַלּוֹן Space ship (chah-lah-leet) חֲלָלִית, Cat (chah-tool) ול
ט	Tet	9	Lamb (tah-lay) טָלֶה, Castle (tee-rah) טִירָה Pilot (tah-yahs) טַיָּס, Tasty (tah-eem) טָעִים
י	Yud	10	Moon (yah-ray-ah) יָרֵחַ, Dove (yoh-nah) יוֹנָה Boy (yeh-led) יֶלֶד, Girl (yahl-dah) יַלְדָּה
כ	Kaf	20	Dog (keh-lev) כֶּלֶב, Pocket (kees) כִּיס Star (ko-chahv) כּוֹכָב, Chair (kee-say) כִּסֵּא
ל	Lamed	30	Lizard (leh-tah-ah) לְטָאָה, Clown (lay-tzahn) לֵיצָן Learn (loe-mayd) לוֹמֵד, Chalkboard (loo-ahch) לוּחַ
מ	Mem	40	Water (mah-yim) מַיִם, Cave (meh-ah-rah) מְעָרָה Slide (mahg-ley-shah) מַגְלֵשָׁה
נ	Nun	50	Harp (neh-vel) נֵבֶל, Tune (nee-goon) נִגּוּן Bark (no-vay-ahch) נוֹבֵחַ, Tiger (nah-mare) נָמֵר
ס	Samech	60	Ladder (soo-lahm) סֻלָּם, Grandma (sahv-tah) סַבְתָּא Candy (soo-kah-ree-yah) סֻכָּרִיָּה, Story (see-poor) ספּוּר
ע	Ayin	70	Eye (ah-yin) עַיִן, Cake (oo-gah) עוּגָה, Tree (aytz) עֵץ Leaf (ah-lay) עָלֶה, Spider (ah-kah-veesh) עַכָּבִישׁ
פ	Pey	80	Butterfly (pahr-pahr) פַּרְפַּר, Flower (peh-rahch) פֶּרַח Mouth (peh) פֶּה, Elephant (peel) פִּיל
צ	Tzadik	90	Submarine (tzo-leh-leht) צוֹלֶלֶת, Turtle (tsahv) צָב Yellow (tzah-hove) צָהֹב, Frog (tsfahr-day-ah) צְפַרְדֵּעַ
ק	Koof	100	Monkey (kofe) קוֹף, Magic (keh-sem) קֶסֶם Rhinoceros (kahr-nahf) קַרְנַף, Nest (ken) קֵן
ר	Raish	200	Wind (roo-ach) רוּחַ, Wet (rah-tove) רָטֹב Run (rahtz) רָץ, Train (rah-keh-vet) רַכֶּבֶת
ש	Shin	300	Sleep (shay-nah) שֵׁנָה, Sun (sheh-mesh) שֶׁמֶשׁ Clock (shah-one) שָׁעוֹן, Blanket (smee-chah) שְׂמִיכָה
ת	Taf	400	Palm (tah-mahr) תָּמָר, Parrot (too-key) תֻּכִּי Goat (tie-eesh) תַּיִשׁ, Drum (tofe) תֹּף